THE
MILITARY

DEFENDING THE NATION

Eloise Paananen

A Blackbirch Graphics Book

RSVP

RAINTREE STECK-VAUGHN
P U B L I S H E R S

Austin, Texas

A Blackbirch Graphics Book

Printed and bound in Mexico

1 2 3 4 5 6 7 8 9 0   RRD   98 97 96 95 94 93

Library of Congress Cataloging-in-Publication Data

Paananen, Eloise.
      The military: defending the nation/ written by Eloise Paananen.
          p.   cm.— (Good citizenship library)
      Includes bibliographical information and index.
      Summary: Surveys the military's role in the history of the United States and discusses how the military works, what it does in peace and war, the chain of command, the draft, the Pentagon, and other related topics.
      ISBN 0-8114-7353-8   ISBN 0-8114-5581-5 (softcover)
      1. United States—Armed Forces—History—Juvenile literature.
[1. United States—Armed Forces] I. Title. II. Series.
UA23.P214 1992
349.73—dc20
355'.00973—dc20   92-29008
                                                     CIP
                                                     AC

Acknowledgments and Photo Credits

Cover: © Bill Swersey/Gamma Liaison; p. 4: © Mike Okoniewski/Gamma Liaison; p. 7: © Bruce Glassman; pp. 11, 12, 15, 38: The Library of Congress; p. 17: North Wind Picture Archives; pp. 18, 19, 20: AP/Wide World Photos; p. 22: © Adam Jahiel/Gamma Liaison; p. 25: Ken Hammond, USAF, Department of Defense; p. 29: © R. Rolle/Gamma Liaison; pp. 30, 33, 35: Wide World Photos; p. 36: Department of Defense; p. 39: © Yves Debay/Gamma Liaison; p. 40: © Noel Quida/Gamma Liaison; p. 45 © Richard Vogel/Gamma Liaison.

Photo research by Grace How

Contents

The Military

in Our World

 The military of the United States is
made up of the Army, Navy, Air Force,
and the Marines. The National Guard
and the U.S. Reservists are civilians
who officially become part of the military during
war. In addition, the U.S. Coast Guard, which is
part of the Transportation Department in peacetime, becomes part of the Navy in wartime. The
military also maintains a special police force and
intelligence departments. Today's U.S. military
"complex" includes a large nuclear force of missiles
and bombs that have come to replace humans in
the country's combined military strength. But the
character of our military is still determined by the
officers, combat soldiers, pilots, engineers, and

Opposite:
**Nearly every
nation in the
world has a
military. A
military serves
to protect and
defend the
interests of its
homeland.**

many other technicians and specialists who make up the armed forces of the United States.

The Army is trained to fight on land. The Navy is responsible for handling conflicts on sea. Military operations by air are carried out by the Air Force. The Marines are trained to fight both at sea and on land. They may travel with the Navy to land and fight ground wars at battle fronts.

The Role of the Military

The military exists to fight. But in the modern world it also serves another, more symbolic, role. Nearly every country in the world has some form of military, even though few nations plan or want to enter a war. For many people, their military is a symbol of potential strength: Their military forces send the message to other countries that they are equipped to defend themselves and even attack if need be.

Like most governments, the United States pays to train, equip, and keep its military at the ready to protect its freedom and its nationhood. As an active member of the United Nations, and as one of the most powerful democratic countries in the world, it is also sometimes called upon to defend the liberties of other countries.

Public Opinion

American citizens by and large understand that the United States must maintain a military. And they expect the best from our armed forces. Some, however, criticize the military's role when the United States seems not to be directly endangered by a war. Why, these Americans ask, should U.S. troops be involved in other countries' wars? To critics, the riots in Los Angeles in 1992 proved that the country needs an organized armed force, such as the National Guard, to control civil disturbances at home.

Those who support a foreign peacetime role for U.S. troops answer that the United States is part of a larger world. What happens in other countries will affect us sooner or later, they say. In the 1930s, many people thought that Adolf Hitler's actions in central Europe were "none of our business." But

The United Nations has a peacekeeping force, which is a military made up of soldiers from many different member countries. They work together to try to solve international conflicts. The U.N. head-quarters is located in New York City.

more and more countries were attacked or got involved. Soon there was a major world war. After World War II, the United Nations was founded to prevent another war like it from happening again. This union of countries decided that if one nation or its leaders started to violate the rights of other nations or of its own people, the other nations of the world would have a responsibility to stop it. This is what U.N. members believed they were doing when they used force to make Iraq get out of Kuwait in 1991. It is also what the United States believed it was doing when it invaded Panama in 1989 to depose the local ruler, Manuel Noriega, who was accused of supporting a network of illegal drug smugglers.

International agreements also exist to protect the right of any country's ships and planes to travel peaceably through parts of the world that belong to no nation—the open seas and much of the air. If one country violates such an agreement, the United Nations can call on its member nations to use force to restore the world's open regions. That was another argument that was used to justify the action against Iraq in 1991—that Iraq was closing off a vital water-way (the Persian Gulf) to international shipping.

That foreign involvement by the U.S. military serves the long-term interests of this country is a practical argument for the military's actions. But there is another argument, too. It is that there are certain principles that all civilized people recognize, and rights that all people possess. If anyone's rights are violated, this argument goes, everybody's rights are potentially in danger.

For either or both of these reasons, many people feel that the military's role is not only to fight when there is a war, but to prevent wars from breaking out if it can. To do that, this country needs military troops and the will to use them. Many people believe history shows that if an enemy knows a nation is able and willing to fight, it is less likely to do something that would provoke a fight.

Continuing Need of the Military

In planning the future role of the military, the government will need to remember that even in the past the armed forces have done other things besides fight, and that new opportunities for service may arise. New troops will have to be trained and equipped, and existing ones will need to upgrade their skills and equipment. Intelligence forces must keep an eye on potential trouble spots and apply advanced technology to prevent open hostilities. Natural disasters such as earthquakes, floods, and hurricanes will still require the military to maintain law and order and to help out victims of the crisis.

Military efforts have had positive effects in civilian spheres as well. Devices and techniques developed for military use have been used in space exploration, for example. Military installations also provide many jobs for civilians.

The Military in

Our History

 The U.S. military as we know it today came into existence gradually through history. The government shaped the military as events within this country's borders and in the world were believed to threaten our safety and well-being.

The Colonial Militia

When America's lands were colonies of Great Britain, there was no formal army or defense force. The main threat to their safety came from clashes with Native American groups that viewed colonists as invaders. A quarter of the early English colony in Virginia had lost their lives in battles with Native Americans. But because their relations with Native

Opposite: **America's first formal army was organized to fight the Revolutionary War and was headed by the first general, George Washington.**

11

Americans had on the whole been peaceful, the colonists hired small civilian forces, called militia, as the need for defense arose.

Beginning in 1637, when the colonists of New England fought against the local Pequot Indians, through the mid-1800s, these militia would range the frontiers, patrol between outposts, and give early warning of any Indian attack.

The colonists basically tolerated English rule until George III became king in 1760. Before long he was in trouble with the colonies over taxes.

Britain had defeated France in the Seven Years' War, which ended in 1763. As a result, Britain had one of the largest empires in the world and with it the biggest debt. To decrease the debt, it was decided that the colonies would pay one-third of the cost to keep about 10,000 British soldiers on American soil. In 1765, Great Britain passed the Stamp Act, which would have taxed about 50 items imported by the colonists.

As colonial resentment of Great Britain grew, the colonists began to think about using force against the British forces stationed in America. In 1774, patriots of the colonies created a select militia force. The force was called the Minutemen because they got ready for battle at a minute's notice.

The battle at Concord bridge was one of the first major battles of the Revolution.

The military revolt against Great Britain began on April 19, 1775, when the "shot heard 'round the world" was fired in the Battle of Lexington and Concord. In the battle that followed, more than 200 British soldiers were killed or wounded.

An Army for the Revolutionary War

On June 17, the New England Army fought its first battle of the war. Some 2,200 British regulars, under the command of General Sir William Howe, assaulted at least as many colonial militiamen dug in on Bunker and Breed's hills near Boston.

Three days before the Battle of Bunker Hill, the Continental Congress, meeting in Philadelphia, had passed a resolution that authorized the American Continental Army. The next day they appointed George Washington to lead the army.

Four major generals were appointed to serve under Washington. All of the colonies promised to help finance the army.

September 1775 saw the beginnings of a navy. Massachusetts Colonel John Glover, acting at Washington's suggestion, armed some fishing vessels, which he manned with fishermen turned sea fighters. The next month, Congress made the navy official, authorizing the fitting out and arming of naval ships. In November, Congress authorized the creation of a marine battalion and drew up rules for the fledgling navy. In December, the first naval officers were commissioned, headed by Esek

Hopkins of Rhode Island, who was given the rank of commodore.

When the Declaration of Independence, written by Thomas Jefferson, was signed in July 1776, there was no turning back. As Benjamin Franklin said, "Gentlemen, we must all hang together, or most assuredly we shall all hang separately." The Continental Army was enlarged as it prepared itself for a long war.

The Army and the U.S. Constitution

After the Revolutionary War, Congress's first military task was to pay off the troops who had fought for independence. With that accomplished, it considered what sort of military establishment the new country should have. The American ideal was a militia of citizen-soldiers. Real conditions, however, demanded at least a small regular force to protect the country's borders (the British still had forts in the Northwest) and to "awe the Indians."

In 1784, Congress officially disbanded most of the existing force and authorized the creation of a small regular army for these purposes. The states still continued to maintain their local militias.

Under the Constitution, this two-fold army structure was kept. That is, Congress could tax to maintain an army and navy, and it could declare war. But the states trained their own militia and appointed their officers. Congress could, however, exercise control over the militia when it called them up in emergencies. The Constitution also made the president commander-in-chief of the armed forces. Congress created a Department of War to advise and assist him in that capacity.

The Role of the First U.S. Military

In the early years of the country's history, a small regular army, supplemented at need by called-up militia and volunteers, patrolled the western frontier. At first, there was no navy, though General Washington had urged the necessity of a naval force to protect American shipping. During the administration of President John Adams (1797–1801), attacks on American ships by the navy of revolutionary France caused Congress to establish a Navy and the U.S. Marine Corps. The new Navy won several engagements with French ships. But when relations between the countries improved, an economy-minded Congress sold off most of its ships for revenue.

The Army fared better. In 1802, Congress created the Corps of Engineers and the Military Academy at West Point. And it was two Army officers, Captain Meriwether Lewis and Lieutenant William Clark, whom President Thomas Jefferson chose to head the expedition to examine the vast Louisiana Territory that the United States had just purchased from France. They were the first of many military personnel who had an important role in the development of America's western territories.

Members of the military have performed many special tasks for our nation. In the 1800s, Army Captain Meriwether Lewis and Lieutenant William Clark explored the Louisiana Territory for President Thomas Jefferson.

The War of 1812

The War of 1812 was fought with Britain over the rights of American vessels to sail the open seas. The U.S. Army saw a mixture of defeats and victories over the next two years. The American campaigns around Detroit as well as an attempted invasion of Canada proved disastrous. But the small Navy, again helped by privateers, seriously disabled British shipping off New England. The victory of the *U.S.S. Constitution* over the British *Guerriére* off Nova Scotia helped to counter the bad news of the fall of Detroit.

After the War of 1812, the Army and Navy were once again reduced. But this time, the Navy was shortly put back into action. American shipping vessels were once more being raided by rulers of North Africa. Stephen Decatur, now a captain, was sent out; he compelled the Barbary states, as they were called, to leave American shipping alone once and for all.

The Mexican War

Besides occasional campaigns against the Indians, the U.S. military was not called upon to fight again until 1845, when the annexation of Texas (which had earlier revolted from Mexico) caused Mexico to attack U.S. forces in the Southwest. The Mexican War served as a proving ground for many officers who would later lead both sides in the Civil War. It also greatly increased the size of the United States.

The Civil War

For the next 15 years, the Army helped survey the West, fought the Indians, and guarded the trails used by pioneer wagons heading west. But the country was being divided by the conflict over slavery and states' rights. In 1861, the Civil War began at Fort Sumter in South Carolina.

Graduates of West Point Academy served on both sides. Indeed, in some cases members of the same family were on different sides.

In many ways, the Civil War was the first of the modern wars: troops were moved by railroad, messages sent by telegraph; Mathew Brady took photographs of battle scenes; and the sea battle of the two ironclad vessels the *Monitor* and the mighty *Merrimac* was a sign of things to come in naval warfare. Many of the generals in the Civil War were

The Battle of Gettysburg was one of the bloodiest and most decisive engagements of the Civil War.

masters of strategy and tactics, and their plans and campaigns would provide textbook examples for future generations of soldiers.

The Spanish-American War

In these same years, as the Navy was reorganized, it replaced its wooden vessels with steel ones. (Steam had already replaced sail for military use.) As new military theories stressing the importance of a strong navy became more popular, the U.S. naval strength increased. A worldwide navy now needed coaling stations—islands where the ships could take on coal for their furnaces—and so the United States became involved in far-off places. In the Spanish-American War (1898), the Navy played a leading role, and afterward helped defend the foreign possessions (Hawaii, the Philippines) that the United States had acquired. By 1900, the United States had the third largest navy in the world.

World War I

In World War I (1914–1918) the United States made an enormous military effort. Total Army enrollment went from 200,000 to almost 4 million. This was a new kind of warfare, which no one had expected: troops were dug down into trenches, while powerful artillery bombardments turned the barren land in front of them into "no man's land." Airplanes were used, first to scout enemy positions, but later in combat with enemy planes and finally

World War I saw the first use of trench warfare, which was combined with destructive bombardment campaigns on land.

on bombing missions. Poison gas and tanks made their appearance, and at sea the Germans' use of submarines against neutral shipping caused America to enter the war.

World War II

World War II saw the rise to prominence of the air arm, which eventually became a separate branch, the Air Force. But the Army, Navy, and Marines maintained their own air services.

It also saw the development of nuclear weapons, and raised important ethical questions about the use of powerful and far-reaching weapons that had destructive capabilities far greater than anything ever imagined. After Germany had surrendered to the Allied powers (the United States, Great Britain, the Soviet Union, and other sympathetic countries), Japan was still fighting against them. In 1945, the United States dropped atomic bombs for the first time on the Japanese cities of Hiroshima and Nagasaki. The level of destruction these bombs caused had never been seen before.

War in the Age of Nuclear Arms: Korea and Vietnam

The "police action" in which United Nations forces, including a sizable American contingent, defended South Korea from a North Korean invasion (1950–1953) gave America a taste of the new kind of warfare that would mark the latter half

On June 6, 1944 (D-Day), American troops helped to turn the tide of World War II by invading Europe on the beaches of Normandy, France.

The Vietnam War (1964–1973) was one of the longest and most un-popular wars in America's history.

of the 20th century. The bomb existed, but no one dared to use it.

Vietnam would be an even worse example of this type of warfare. The United States actively fought to defend the South Vietnamese from Communist North Vietnam from 1964 to 1973. There, the great difficulty of trying to distinguish noncombatant civilians from enemy guerrillas proved frustrating to soldiers at the front. Efforts to use technology to break the stalemate led to more problems, as people became concerned about the environmental and long-term effects of chemicals used to destroy jungle plant cover (Agent Orange, for instance). Because of the frustrations of the war and opposition at home, the United States finally withdrew its troops from Vietnam as battles still raged and no victory was declared.

Strategic Operations

Since the end of the Vietnam War, the U.S. military has limited its involvement in conflicts around the world mostly to stationing nonaggressive troops and carrying out brief and highly strategic (carefully planned) operations. On December 20, 1989, U.S. troops invaded Panama and overthrew the corrupt

★★★★★ The Military Melting Pot ★★★★★

One of the most successful working relationships between the races in America has been in the military. During World War II, despite being in largely segregated units, minorities played an important role: Native Americans proved invaluable as they sent code messages in their native tongues; Japanese Americans served honorably in Italy; and African Americans formed a famous air squadron from Tuskegee, Alabama, that bravely fought the enemy.

The racial integration of the military began in 1948, when most of American society was still strictly segregated. During the Korean War, African-American and white troops fought side by side in integrated units.

Black National Guard units had survived in a few states since the Reconstruction (1867–1877) period following the Civil War. In 1946, New Jersey became the first state to officially integrate its Guard, two years before the integration of the active army. But many states in the Deep South with large African-American populations had all-white Guard units. In 1956, President Dwight D. Eisenhower federalized the entire Arkansas National Guard for a month to prevent the segregationist governor from using it to stop the court-ordered integration of Little Rock High School.

The scene was replayed in 1962 during the desegregation of the University of Mississippi. This time, Guardsmen obeyed President John F. Kennedy. Prodded by the National Guard Bureau, the states began to recruit more African Americans and minorities. The Civil Rights Act of 1965 cemented a fully integrated military. By 1984, minorities made up 26.4 percent of the Guard and almost 10 percent of its officer corps.

Today, minorities attend the military academies and serve in all armed services, on land, in the air, and on the seas. The Marine Corps, the Military Police, Special Forces, the Coast Guard, the Honor Guard are all distinctive services that are well served by African Americans.

government of Panama's president, Manuel Noriega. Noriega surrendered within two weeks.

In 1991, U.S. forces, along with other U.N. forces, fought Iraq after it invaded Kuwait. The conflict ended within three months.

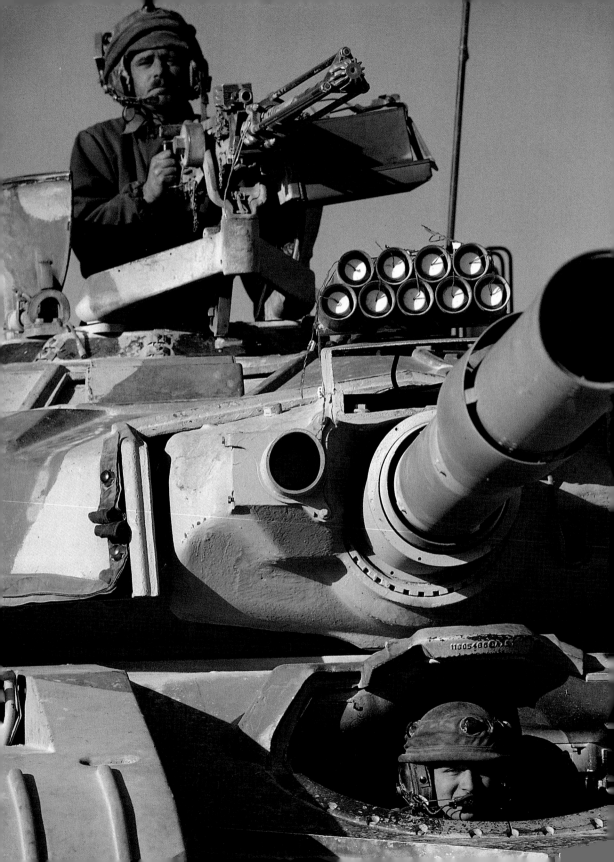

How the

Military Works

Because the U.S. military is under civilian control, the president of the country is commander-in-chief of the armed forces. Normally, the president exercises control through the Department of Defense, one of the 14 departments in the cabinet, which is the president's special group of advisers. Fourteen defense agencies and three military departments report to the Department of Defense: the Department of the Army, the Department of the Navy (which also controls the Marine Corps), and the Department of the Air Force. The U.S. Coast Guard reports either to the Department of Transportation in peacetime or to the Department of the Navy in war.

Opposite:
A complex chain of command guides every move that is made by any branch of the U.S. military.

The Chain of Command

Each military department has its own chief of staff, appointed by the president: the Army Chief of Staff, the Air Force Chief of Staff, the Chief of Naval Operations, and the Commandant of the Marine Corps. The chiefs of staff are the highest-ranking officers in the armed services. Together they make up the Joint Chiefs of Staff, which advises the Department of Defense on all matters of national security and military operations. The Joint Chiefs of Staff can only advise the Department of Defense, however. The secretary of defense, the highest-ranking member of the defense department, has more power than even the chairman of the Joint Chiefs of Staff in deciding matters of national defense. But it is the president who has the final word in activating the military.

The Pentagon and Personnel

All military and defense agencies have their offices in a large complex of buildings in Washington, D.C., called the Pentagon. Just as we say "the White House," meaning the president, or "Capitol Hill," meaning Congress, we often refer to the entire defense establishment as "the Pentagon."

The military departments have the task of recruiting, training, and equipping their forces. Almost 5 million people, including active-duty service members, civilian employees, and Reserve forces, make up the Department of Defense. About

2 million are on active duty with the Army, Navy, Marines, and Air Force. America has 631 military installations and properties; about 435 are in the United States, and 136 are overseas in 20 different countries around the world.

The majority of people in the armed forces are enlisted personnel, noncommissioned officers, or persons with special skills. The different services have different names for some of them, and the specialties differ from service to service.

Those who direct and give commands on a higher level are called commissioned officers. Most often, they are graduates of one of the service academies, officer candidate schools, or the Reserve Officers' Training Corps (ROTC) program in colleges and universities.

The Pentagon, in Washington, D.C., is the administrative headquarters of all U.S. military and defense agencies.

Military Rank

Officer ranks in the Army, Air Force, and Marines begin with second lieutenant and proceed upward through first lieutenant, captain, major, lieutenant colonel, colonel, brigadier general (one star), major general (two stars), lieutenant general (three stars), and general (four stars). The special rank of General of the Army or General of the Air Force (five stars), equivalent to the European field marshal, was created during World War II, and was held by only five men (Henry A. "Hap" Arnold of the Air Force and Omar N. Bradley, Dwight D. Eisenhower, Douglas MacArthur, and George C. Marshall of the Army). Another special rank, "General of the Armies of the United States," was given, after their deaths, to George Washington and to the World War I leader John J. Pershing.

In the Navy, the officer ranks begin at ensign and advance to lieutenant junior grade, lieutenant, lieutenant commander, commander, captain, commodore, rear admiral, vice admiral, and admiral. Commodores and admirals are called flag officers.

Special Troops

In all services, too, there are special groupings of troops that perform specific functions. There are medical corps, who take care of sick and wounded personnel. Maintenance crews service and repair equipment. And there are special forces that almost defy description: the Navy's SEAL (sea, air, land) teams are trained to detonate mines in hostile waters. They also land in enemy territory to see what sort of resistance may be waiting if U.S. troops should invade at that place.

The Draft

Historically, the United States has reduced the number of soldiers in the military during peacetime. When the armed forces enter a war, they often need many more people. Since the Civil War, the size of the forces has been increased in wartime by the draft—a command that able-bodied young men must serve in the military. During the Vietnam War, all male U.S. citizens and permanent residents between the ages of 18 and 26 were assigned numbers. Those whose numbers were drawn in a sort of lottery were required to report for military duty. Not reporting in when called was against the law. The last military draft ended in 1973.

Military service as an "honorable profession" is a subject for debate, particularly for those who are "conscientious objectors." There are those who love their country, but because of religious and moral beliefs refuse to take up firearms. In wartime, these people can legally protest, but must also perform some humanitarian service. Since there is no longer a draft in America, and there are actually too many volunteers for all the services, those who don't want to join the military don't have to.

The National Guard is one of the oldest continuing institutions in this country. It is many years older than the United States itself, many years older than the U.S. Army, and far older than the U.S. Air Force. Citizen-soldiers like those in the National Guard have fought in every major American war since the Pequot War in Connecticut in 1637. Today's National Guard is the equivalent of the Revolutionary War militia—citizen-soldiers who were called up from their civilian jobs whenever and wherever they were needed, under the Constitution's mandate to "provide for the common Defense."

The National Guard is composed of Army or Air Force combat units, each one under the command of the governor of its home state. The units are in either the Army or the Air National Guard. (The Navy and Marine Corps have Reserves, but not National Guard Units.) If the national government thinks a local problem is getting out of hand, the National Guard may be mobilized—it becomes part of the active Army or Air Force and serves under the command of the president of the United States. This may also happen in time of war, as it did during Operation Desert Storm.

The Reservists are units and individuals who, like the National Guard, are part-time soldiers; but they are not part of the state organization the way the National Guard units are. Besides the Army and the Air Force, the Navy, and Marine Corps also have special units of Reservists.

In the Spanish-American War, it had become apparent that there was a serious shortage of military physicians. To remedy this, the Congress passed a law in 1908 establishing the Medical Reserve Corps. In 1916, with World War I raging in Europe and a probability that the United States would be drawn in, Woodrow Wilson signed the National Defense Act. It completely reorganized the War Department and created the Officers' Reserve Corps and the Enlisted Reserve Corps, and established the modern Reserve Officers' Training Corps.

The Reservists would serve in increasing numbers in the wars of the 20th century. Some 200,000 Reservists served in World War II. In Operation Desert Storm, the support Reserves proved to be easily trained and capable of quick mobilization. Their efforts proved uniquely valuable in ending the conflict quickly and victoriously.

Joining Up

There are many jobs of many kinds in the military. They range from cook to paratrooper, radar communications or electronics technician to flight mechanic. In some branches, enlisted personnel may qualify for commissions through further training. A person may also choose to join the Regular or Reserve Army, Navy, Air Force, or Marines, or the Army or Air National Guard.

Young people can enlist between the ages of 18 (17 with the consent of one's parents) and 34. Enlistees must have a high-school diploma. If they have not yet graduated, they can enlist if they can produce a letter from their school certifying that they will graduate that year. They must also pass the physical examination. Enlistees go through basic training (8 weeks in the Army) and then take from 3 to 23 weeks of advanced training.

Enlisted Guard personnel who wish to become officers must take an Officer's Candidate School Test. If they pass, they are sent to an officer candidate school in their home state; their time there takes the place of weekend training sessions. Another route to officer status is to participate in the Reserve Officers' Training Corps program while attending a college or university; from there, one can go into the Regulars, or the Reserves, or the National Guard. National Guard personnel who wish to join the Regulars or the Reserves are reclassified and take a reduction in grade.

The National Guard was called into service to help restore order to Los Angeles in 1992 when urban rioting destroyed part of the city.

4

What the Military

Does in War

The military may have duties in peacetime, but its ultimate purpose is waging war. The Constitution gives Congress the power to declare war, but makes the president commander-in-chief of the armed forces. Presidents in the past have used their power to involve U.S. troops without a formal declaration of war by Congress. To prevent this, the War Powers Resolution of 1973 was passed to maintain the balance between Congress and the president in matters of war. Under this resolution, the president cannot commit troops to action for more than 90 days without the formal approval of Congress. In the Gulf War, President George Bush made sure he had Congress's approval.

Opposite:
American army jeeps roll across the desert sands during the Persian Gulf War in 1991.

31

Preparing for War

An old saying goes, "In time of peace, prepare for war." At the Pentagon, the military is always preparing for possible wars. Studies are made and strategies are planned for ways of coping with any possible problems. Officers meet regularly to discuss and evaluate the information received from security agencies, the State Department, overseas embassies, the White House, and the members and staff of the armed forces committees of Congress. It all comes under the general heading of "contingency planning," which simply means, "What if...?" Contingency planning is meant to enable the military to deal with such questions as where and how the many troops are to be located, what weapons will be available, how to transport troops and supplies to support a war, and how to win quickly with the fewest injuries and the least loss of life. These plans must also take into account the plans of allies and the weaknesses of potential enemies.

In both planning and waging war, modern forces have the help of technology. But, they must also take into account the technology of possible enemies. Both sides, for example, may have satellites swirling in space, keeping an eye on what's going on. Technology has changed the very nature of war, introducing such offensive and defensive weapons as "smart bombs" that can spot their own targets, computer-guided missiles, and, of course, the nuclear bomb. Aircraft fly from carriers or from bases thousands of miles away from their targets, and are commanded by computerized systems. Submarines are powered by nuclear energy. Secrecy, and the possibility of surprise that goes with it, are important parts of a war plan, but today modern communications can bring battlefield operations into the living rooms of friend and foe alike.

When War Is Declared

Once war is declared, the country is alerted. The choice of commanders is crucial. Much depends on their previous experience in war. The different services have a history of friendly rivalry that can sometimes hamper operations. It is essential that someone be in charge: There must be a unified command of operations, which coordinates the tasks of the different services.

The Persian Gulf War

Operation Desert Storm, the combined U.N. action to eject Iraqi forces from Kuwait in 1991, is a model example of how the U.S. military engages in warfare today. The war lasted only 43 days. But it was fought after years of careful planning. As early as 1988, U.S. General H. Norman Schwarzkopf, then commander-in-chief of the U.S. central command, had started contingency planning for a conflict in the Middle East.

At 2 p.m. on August 2, 1990, Iraqi forces burst across the border invading Kuwait. In the air were

General Norman Schwarzkopf commanded American troops in the Persian Gulf War and masterminded the military strategy that defeated Iraq.

Soviet-built MIG fighter planes. Several hundred Soviet-supplied T-72 tanks, along with the large 140,000-man invasion force, took Kuwait City, street by street. The Kuwaitis resisted, but could not push the enemy back.

Because of the planning the United States had done beforehand, General Schwarzkopf was able to begin positioning his forces within five days. By August 27, command headquarters had been established in the Saudi Arabian capital of Riyadh, and three divisions and the 3rd Armored Cavalry (made up of tanks) were being transported to the northern part of that country. In addition to the full-time career members of the armed forces, President Bush authorized the call-up of 1 million members of the National Guard and Reserves for service of up to two years.

Not all these people would be needed to fight, if it came to fighting. A modern military operation requires great numbers of people in many support positions: cooks and doctors and nurses, vehicle service mechanics, communication technicians, and linguists. The personnel even included cultural advisers—Americans had to be warned that certain gestures that are perfectly ordinary in America are deadly insults in the Middle East.

Modern Battle

On January 16, 1991 (in Washington; it was early morning of January 17 in the Middle East), the

The highly sophisticated technology of the Stealth bomber performs risky operations with great success.

Allies began to bombard Iraq with bombs and missiles. The explosives were delivered by some very advanced, "high-tech" systems. Using geographical information obtained from several satellites in orbit, Tomahawk missiles were able to follow the contours of the land to find their programmed targets. Special aircraft flying as much as 100 miles from the target area broadcast signals that confused the electronic homing devices in Iraqi surface-to-air missiles (SAMs) so that they couldn't find Allied planes and missiles coming in. The U.S. Stealth bomber, which had performed poorly in Panama, this time managed to hit most of its targets.

The Iraqis also had some high-tech weapons. On the first day of the bombardment, seven Iraqi Scud missiles were launched at Israel. The Allies countered these with their Patriot missiles, which intercepted a Scud over Dhahran and later were placed in Israel to protect that country from further attacks by Iraqi missiles.

★★★★★ General Colin L. Powell, ★★★★★ Chairman of the Joint Chiefs of Staff

General Colin L. Powell was appointed the twelfth chairman of the Joint Chiefs of Staff, Department of Defense, by President George Bush in August 1989. He was reappointed for a second term in October 1991. He was the first African-American officer to receive this distinguished honor.

General Powell was born in New York City in 1937 and was raised in the South Bronx. His illustrious career has included military duty in Korea and Vietnam as well as in Germany. He is a former commander of the elite 101st Airborne Division. He holds a master's degree in business administration as well as a number of other honors from advanced military training institutions. He has been highly decorated by the military services and is currently serving his second term as principal military advisor to the president. During the Persian Gulf War, General Powell and Secretary of Defense Richard Cheney oversaw the conflict from Washington and worked closely with General Schwarzkopf on battle plans and strategies.

Many supporters have suggested that General Powell run for political office on his retirement, but he

General Colin L. Powell

claims he has no such plans. General Powell is married to Alma Vivian Johnson, and they have three children; Michael, Linda, and Annemarie.

Public Opinion About War

In the end, a war requires weapons that work and trained troops who know how to make use of those weapons. But it also requires something else. The troops, and the people back home, must believe in the cause they are fighting for. In war, lives are lost, people are wounded, sadness and tragedy strike many families. Although little can make up for the death of a loved one, those who survive must believe the loss was for a just cause.

The Gulf War and the American Public

Many Americans considered Operation Desert Storm a victory for our military and for justice in the world. But others criticized our involvement in the war. They complained that we used violence when we might have used more peaceful means to stop Iraq's leader, Saddam Hussein. One method we had used with Iraq and other countries before was trade embargoes, or restrictions on a country's right to import and export products that could be vital to its survival. People opposed to the war also pointed out that the destruction it had caused would affect us all for years to come. For example, oil spills in the Persian Gulf caused by the war were a major global environmental hazard.

Every war creates mixed feelings. But the Persian Gulf War proved that the United States today could fight a war quickly and successfully, with a minimum of casualties on either side.

Molly Pitcher

Military women are justly proud of their service, which began in America during the 1778 Battle of Monmouth. Molly Pitcher helped to fight the British when her husband, John Hays, an artilleryman, was wounded. Until that moment she had moved among the weary, parched soldiers with her water pitcher, dispensing water, binding wounds, and giving encouragement. When she saw the troops lying mutilated and her husband unable to fire a cannon, she put down her water pitcher, grabbed the ramming staff, and swabbed out the hot cannon barrel with water to extinguish sparks and remove unexploded powder. She then rammed home a charge and fired, staying at her station as rammer until relieved by a trained artilleryman.

During the 18th and 19th centuries, women were routinely present with armies in battle. It was not unusual for respectable wives and daughters to go along with their men. The Army authorized three to six per company to draw rations for themselves and their children in return for their services, including cooking, sewing, and laundry. Army nurses were also always needed.

During the Civil War, some 400 women served on both sides; many were spies. Loreta Velásquez from Cuba, bought a Confederate uniform, glued on a moustache and chin beard, and recruited a troop of soldiers. She fought in a number of battles, including Bull Run. Unmasked, she then went into the cavalry. Widowed twice, she headed west in search of gold.

Many women volunteered for the Army Nurse Corps in World War I, but were not considered fully part of the Army. But the Navy, needing personnel for clerical tasks, found that the legislation authorizing it to recruit members just required "persons." It offered women the opportunity to join as Naval Reserve Yeomen. (Yeomen are petty officers who perform noncombat jobs.) The Coast Guard and the Marines also had female yeomen.

In World War II, women were again able to serve in noncombatant jobs. The Women's Army Auxiliary Corps (WAAC) was formed in 1942, but its status was unclear, and in 1943 it was disbanded and the Women's Army Corps (WAC) formed to take its place. In 1942, an act of Congress authorized the Navy to enlist and grant commissions to women, who were organized as Women Accepted for Volunteer Emergency Services (WAVES) in the U.S. Naval Reserve. There were also many women in the Coast Guard, called SPAR (from the Coast Guard motto, *Semper paratus*, "Always ready), and the Marine Corps.

A small (about 1,000) but skilled group of women in World War II were members of the Women's Air Force Service Pilots (WASP), headed by Jacqueline Cochran. Though officially civilians under civil service, they ferried planes from factories to air bases, towed target planes for Army-Air corpsmen to shoot at, and tested new and experimental planes that regular pilots wouldn't touch.

In 1948, congressional legislation authorized the creation of women's units in all the branches of military service. During the 1970s, women were increasingly brought into the mainstream of military life. They were admitted to the service academies (West Point, Annapolis, the Air Force Academy), and for a few years they even took basic training with men. In 1978, the WAC was officially disbanded and women integrated into the regular and Reserve units of the Army. A woman became the captain of the Corps of Cadets at West Point in 1989.

Meanwhile, special legislation allowed women to join the National Guard and Reserves. As more jobs within the military were opened to women, the number of women in both the Army and Air National Guard rose dramatically.

Today men and women work and train together, and more than 90 percent of the Army's jobs are open to women.

A female army soldier operates a machine gun.

What the Military

Does in Peace

During peacetime, the military remains busy keeping itself fully trained, up to date, and prepared for any crisis. Training in all kinds of skills and activities keeps military men and women active. Each person wants to excel, to move forward in a career that asks for vigilance while awaiting orders from superiors. The military salute's message is, "We are ready. Give the command."

Disaster Relief

The Air Force's Aerospace Rescue and Recovery Service and the Coast Guard rescue those in peril in the air, on land, and on sea. All services are trained to help with disaster relief following earthquakes,

Opposite: **Providing aid to countries in need is one of the military's most important noncombat functions. Here, food and medical supplies are unloaded at the Sarajevo airport, in Bosnia-Herzegovina.**

41

In the 1990s, the military will be decreasing the number of enlisted men and women. As the military comes to rely more on advanced technology, it will also demand highly skilled personnel. "You'll see an increase in people with high school diplomas, people with higher test scores, and a decrease in those with the lowest acceptable standards," says Major General Jack C. Wheeler, head of Army recruiting.

According to the Defense Department, 99 percent of all recruits now have high-school degrees. Test scores have also risen. Five years ago, three out of four who wanted to get into the service could get in. Today one out of four will get in. The Armed Services National Aptitude Battery—the test that measures language, arithmetic, and mechanical aptitudes—may not have changed, but the cutoff point for qualifying has risen.

With the many political changes that occurred during the late 1980s and early 1990s, America began to redefine who potential enemies really are. According to Major General Perry M. Smith (U.S. Air Force, retired), since World War II, American defense efforts concentrated on a single consistent enemy—the USSR. But now, the USSR has dissolved.

General Smith believes that the U.S. military's future role will be less defined, and the national security effort will have to take into account many possible kinds of conflict. Two areas that could be potential threats today to national security, according to General Smith, are East Asia and Latin America.

The way things are done in the military will change too, as technology makes work easier in some ways with computers, modems, and laser printers. By the turn of the century, many people envision automatic dictation machines and computerized data storage and retrieval systems that will change workloads and working hours, making it possible to analyze messages and produce reports more quickly.

floods, and any civil disorder. The Air Force is frequently called upon to supply food and shelter and carry medical personnel to distressed areas.

Medical doctors, nurses, and technicians are flown

in to help in these crises. Marine helicopters, for example, flew supplies to the desperate Kurds in Iraq following Operation Desert Storm, and in 1992, were involved in the relief efforts in Bosnia when Yugoslavia's republics were ravaged by civil war.

Civic Aid

The National Guard, which is always stationed at home in peacetime, helps in civic projects. It assists local law enforcement and rescue workers during emergencies. Natural disasters, such as volcanic eruptions, floods, forest fires, and earthquakes, find the National Guard on duty to protect life and property. Some states also use the Guard to help prevent illegal drug trafficking. In civil disturbances, such as the Los Angeles rioting and looting in May 1992, the National Guard takes up arms to help restore peace.

Remembering Our Veterans

Displays at the Pentagon and exhibits at museums around the country give people an understanding of history and of the contributions of the military.

Memorial Day and Veterans Day remind all Americans that much is owed to those who have served this nation. Those who have been wounded and are ill are treated for free at veterans' hospitals and related nursing care facilities. The VA (Veterans Administration) provides hundreds of programs for veterans who are young and healthy but because of

Military police are called MPs in the Army and Shore Patrol in the Navy. Their job is similar to that of civilian police forces. They keep people and property safe, enforce traffic and other laws, and take charge of persons who have broken the law after the military court has decided on a punishment.

Court-Martial

If a member of any of the armed services does something that would be a crime for a civilian, or seriously violates a military regulation, he or she may be apprehended by the military police or the Navy's Shore Patrol, and tried by a special system of military courts, under a body of law called the Uniform Code of Military Justice. The court itself is called a court-martial, and the proceedings are called that, too. Unlike civilian courts, which are continuing bodies, a court-martial is convened by the officer in charge as there is need. Most of the usual protections of the law apply: the defendant has the right to have a lawyer, the right to call and cross-examine witnesses, and is considered innocent until proven guilty. The defendant can also appeal the decision of the officers.

Penalties for those found guilty range from confinement to quarters or loss of a month's pay through lowering of rank, loss of pay, discharge from the service, and imprisonment.

Intelligence

The word *intelligence* means "information gathering." The information can be anything from satellite pictures for mapmakers to wiretaps and spying missions. Intelligence is any information that helps the military to better do its job.

Many people think of intelligence in terms of spying by the Central Intelligence Agency (the CIA). But the military has its own information-gathering sources, too. The Air Force National Reconnaissance Office spends most of its annual budget of some $30 billion on electronic eavesdropping systems and sophisticated photographic satellites.

As a result of failures over the past few years to learn what policy makers needed to know, a new organization, the National Human Intelligence Tasking Center, will begin operating very soon. Using secret agents—human beings—rather than fancy hardware may seem like a step back in time, but they are not only cheaper, they are far more effective in learning what is happening in potential trouble spots.

Memorial Day rituals enable Americans to remember the sacrifices and brave deeds of those who have served in our armed forces.

job cutbacks must become civilians and seek jobs. The GI Benefits Act pays for college education, and there is also help for spouses (usually the wives) of those who are killed in action.

The transition from military to civilian life is cushioned by such advantages as home loan assistance, retraining, civil service preference jobs, and a plan in each state for its veterans to get the best possible chance at jobs and care. But more than programs are needed. Serving in the armed forces often means a great disruption in the lives of soldiers. After service is complete, most people require emotional as well as financial assistance to "put their lives back in order." Getting back to work as a civilian, returning to a family, and trying to cope with the harsh memories or injuries of war all take a great deal of time. Emotional support and understanding from those who welcome veterans home is always the most important element in helping those individuals return to leading happy and productive lives.

45

Glossary

battalion   A tactical military unit that usually consists of a headquarters unit and four infantry companies or military batteries (troop units).

commissioned officer   One who directs or gives orders on a high level.

contingency   A possible outcome.

court-martial   Military court and legal proceedings.

draft   Required military service by the government.

expedition   Exploratory trip.

guerrillas   Irregular combat personnel, usually disguised or camouflaged, who strike by surprise.

intelligence   Military information gathering.

militia   Civilian forces that are called upon to fight in times of emergency.

reconnaissance   Military and strategic information gathering; intelligence.

trench warfare   Strategy whereby troops are dug into deep trenches while powerful artillery bombards land between the trenches and the enemy; first used in World War I.

veteran   Person who has served in the military.

yeoman   Petty officer who performs noncombat jobs.

For Further Reading

Baker, D. *Future Fighters.* Vero Beach, FL: Rourke, 1990.

Blue, Rose, and Naden, Corinne J. *Colin Powell: Straight to the Top.* Brookfield, CT: The Millbrook Press, 1991.

Bratman, Fred. *War in the Persian Gulf.* Brookfield, CT: The Millbrook Press, 1991.

Detzer, David. *An Asian Tragedy: America and Vietnam.* Brookfield CT: Millbrook Press, 1992.

Grant, Neil. *Heroes of World War II.* Austin, TX: Raintree Steck-Vaughn, 1991.

Ross, Stewart. *The Origins of World War I.* New York: Franklin Watts, 1989.

Stein, R.C. *D-Day.* Chicago: Childrens Press, 1988.

Index

Index